HOW TO KEEP BEES
WITHOUT FINDING THE QUEEN

I should like to dedicate this book to my wife, Josie, and all my family for there patience over the years. Also to all the beekeepers I have met for there company and friendship.

First published in 2008 by Northern Bee Books,
Scout Bottom Farm, Mytholmroyd, Hebden Bridge.

ISBN 978-1-904846-30-7

The author would like to record his thanks to Jeremy Burbidge of Northern Bee Books for his help and guidance. Also to Jason Salisbury for help in getting the manuscript into publication form.

INTRODUCTION

I have not undertaken the writing of this book lightly. When colleagues have suggested that I write a book on beekeeping I have always said that I would not do this until I had something new to say about my favourite hobby. I have always read anything on bees that has come to hand, as a teenager I read every bee book that the Birmingham Central Library had on their shelves. This included both volumes of "Beekeeping New and Old Described with Pen and Camera" by Herrod Hempsall. These are now collectors items and command good money. I have come to the conclusion that many of the regular bee books are a rehash of the books which the author has read in the past. It may have done the author good but adds little to the knowledge of beekeeping.

Several of the methods contained in this book are the result of trial and error. When something goes wrong I try to do two things, firstly put it right and then see how things can be changed to prevent the problem occurring again. In this way it is possible to make headway and improve one's method of keeping bees.

An example of this is the feeding of colonies. For years I made syrup every autumn, carried it to the colonies and poured it into the feeder. About 10 years ago I realised that my colonies were quite full of stores by the end of September, there is a flow from Heather and Ivy. I also recalled reading a book, where the author had weighed colonies regularly during the winter, the results showed that the consumption of food was very low, only ounces, each month from October until early spring. Once the colony started to rear brood then the food consumption rises in time with this which accounts for the colony losses from starvation during March and April. We see flowers around and assume the colony will be getting sufficient food to maintain the colony. Some food is coming in but the large amount of brood needs much more than this. I have now given up making syrup and do not feed my colonies until the New Year, and then it is fondant.

In my early days we made candy, I recall it took most of Saturday morning and the end product was just a few pounds of candy. The cost was the sugar and the heat. Now you can purchase candy, known as Baker's Fondant for little more than the cost of the sugar, and no physical work involved. My supplier has 12.5 kilo boxes [£11.50 per box in 2006] and I have seen 15 kilo boxes as well, both of these are quite heavy so beware when you collect them. Some is scented so avoid this as it will taint your honey. Look in Yellow Pages under 'Bakers requisites' for a local supplier.

My crown boards are half size; two cover a brood chamber and one a nucleus box. They have pieces of 1 x 1 nailed on the top side, this space will hold 6lbs of fondant and this is then placed upside down on top of the frames, as one gets low another can be put alongside. For me this has worked very well. If you think of going this route do try with a small number of colonies to see that is feasible in your area. The fondant keeps well if the air is excluded from the surface, it can be cut with a large knife or a cheese cutter. Occasionally it goes dry and hard but a spray of water is all that is required.

I hope you find the contents of this book helpful. I am sure some beekeepers take the view that every beekeeper can find queens easily and regularly. You will see that I take a very different view. It is possible to keep bees without the need to find the queen. It just needs a different approach.

I hope you enjoy the book. I am sure some of the ideas will be controversial. I hope you find some of the book useful. Do enjoy your life.

Do enjoy your beekeeping.

UNITS AND MEASUREMENTS

This is still a problem when writing a book. All our bee hives are in Imperial measurement and to convert these to Metric seems a waste of time. In general I have used Imperial units without the Metric equivalents. I suggest you use the following approximate conversions.

Feet and inches. There are 25 millimetres in one inch, so 3 are 1/8th of an inch. One foot is 300 millimetres so multiples are easy 300, 600 [2 feet], 900 [3 feet], and so on.

Weight. 2.2 pounds is one kilo, 1000 kilo is a metric ton. 1000 times 2.2 is 2200 pounds, very close to an Imperial ton. 454 grams is one pound, approx. half a kilo. 454 divided into 16 ounces is approx. 28 grams per ounce.

Volume. A litre is 1 and ¾ pints. A gallon is approx. 4 and ½ litres.

CONTENTS

1	Me and my beekeeping	9
2	The queen, an amazing creature	13
3	Actually finding the queen	17
4	Queen excluders and includers	21
5	Swarming	23
6	Artificial swarming by the Pagden method	27
7	Actually making a 'shook swarm'	33
8	The 'shook swarm' and disease	39
9	Extended possibilities	41
10	Colony production and queen replacement	51
11	Queen rearing	53
12	Keeping bees inside	57
13	Mini-nucs to make	63
14	The future	69

WILFRID MANN 1898-1980.

Bees on display at City of Birmingham flower show in Handsworth park, circa 1960.

Photo courtesy of Birmingham Post and Mail

CHAPTER 1

Me and my beekeeping

My father, Wilfrid Mann, an only son, was born in 1898 at Brockmoor near Brierley Hill in Staffordshire. He was 16 when World War 1 started, after a while he lied about his age and volunteered to join the Staffordshire Regiment. He went to France and was in the trenches in the Somme and at Passchendaele. Fortunately he came back or otherwise this would have to be written by a different author.

My parents married in 1927 and I arrived a while later, a brother arrived two years afterwards. In 1941 my father was working as a bricklayer and was caretaker of the building company for which he worked. We lived on the premises and he had noticed some bees flying in and out under a metal sheet, an old enamelled advert, he was interested and curious. It turned out they were bumble bees. Earlier in his life he had kept white Angora rabbits and Pomeranian dogs. While I was at home we had mice, rabbits, hens, pigeons, budgerigars and foreign birds and a Parrot, not all at once but over the years, in every case my father was keen on showing the current hobby.

Dad bought a book on beekeeping; this was unusual as he was not a great reader. I was given the book to read, I can recall clearly handing it back and saying "Dad this is too complicated, you do it." At the time we were living about a mile from the centre of Birmingham, not really beekeeping country. Mother was a teacher, during the war she was an A.R.P. warden and also collected money for National Saving Stamps, the area manager for this had a timber bungalow near Bewdley about 20 miles from Birmingham. Our family were invited to the bungalow for a weekend; in due course we had a bungalow at the same farm. During a walk in the Wyre forest we found an apiary where the mature gentleman had a row of WBC hives along a fence, we got chatting and eventually we bought a box with 8 B.S brood frames. There was a colony of bees within but it was late in the season and they died out during the winter, lesson one.

By May 1942 my father had joined the Birmingham Beekeepers and arranged to buy a full colony. He made a travelling box and a complete WBC hive, on a Saturday morning my brother and I went across Birmingham by tram and the colony was transferred into the box. On the return journey the bees had to travel on the platform next to the driver, he kept on looking down at them!! We met our parents at Snow hill Station and we all went by train to Bewdley Station, then a three mile walk along the river Severn to the farm. On the Sunday we transferred the bees into the WBC without a sting, later I lay in front on the grass, watching, and was stung above the right eye, another lesson. Over the next few years we built up to five or six colonies. My father got a licence to purchase some timber to make bee hives and also an allowance of petrol to visit the bees. How times have changed.

When I came to leave school there was a careers interview. Mother was there, me and the adviser. I was asked "What is your hobby?" "Beekeeping" I replied," "There's no future in that" came the reply "What else do you do?", "Help my father to repair his car" I replied, end of interview, so I became an apprentice motor mechanic. I hope things have improved. In September I was told to go and enrol at the local Technical College, I had not enjoyed school and was not keen but in due course I did well and became a full time lecturer at another college. This was the "proper job" and beekeeping has been the hobby ever since. I have no complaints. I guess that the adviser was right, I had no experience, was too young, in the wrong area and no capital to start up the project.

In the Birmingham Association there was a gentleman named Mr E.W.T.Morris who was keen on members taking BBKA examinations and I see from my certificates that I took the Preliminary, now called the Basic at the age of 17, the Intermediate at 19, while doing National Service, and the theory papers for the senior at 22. It was not until 20 years later that I was in a position to try the senior practical, the first try was not a success, the exam is very searching, as it should be. Two examiners arrived; one had a chauffeur so that made three. They came at 10.00 AM and left at 4.00 PM. They start off checking all your equipment and methods, then a very through practical in the apiary and lastly some microscope work. Dissecting with six eyes staring at you does not make for an easy time, so I failed. Next year was to be a repeat, this time with two examiners only. Early in the morning I made the dissections and put them safely to one side. The day went much better, then the microscope work, this went very much better, and I had "One I did earlier" available, they were not required. I passed this time.

Over the years I kept up to six colonies until the 1970's then rising to 50 until 1986 and now 10 to 20. About five years ago one of my 'nice nieces' started keeping bees and she was joined by her father, much to my surprise. Dad would have been amazed!! In May 2004 my middle son asked about bees, he had helped a little when a teenager. He was able to take a hived swarm home later that month; there was a crop on 42 pounds of Lime honey in August. I do not think he has been into the brood chamber and this year this one colony produced 145 pounds of the same Lime honey. I must be doing something wrong. I have a jar of his Lime honey, now 18 months old and as clear as a bell, not a sign of granulation.

Beekeeping is like a disease; once you are really hooked it is impossible to stop. I think it has excellent advantages; bees do not need taking for a walk or cleaning out, or feeding every day. Most of the work is in the fine and warm weather and the longer you keep bees the more you realise that there is still so much more to learn.

Once I wasn't
Now I am
And soon I will not be again

Old Chinese quotation

CHAPTER 2

The queen – an amazing creature

I still look into a colony and think "How on earth do they do it?" All those bees in such a small space, how is it possible, how is it all organised? How can they build such beautiful comb in the dark without tools as we would understand them? How do they decide who does what and when, who goes out to collect what and where from. Some of the answers have been found by dedicated researchers but to me it is all still very amazing.

Maybe we people on earth look similar to a bee colony when viewed from outer space, all of us rushing around. When you do see a queen Bee she is so small and yet the colony relies so much on her abilities. She came from a fertile egg and was fed on Royal Jelly. In 16 days she emerged and in 10 to 20 days more she was mated and in lay and would be likely to continue as the colonies queen for the next two to three years. The same egg in a worker cell would have produced a worker bee and her life's work could be completed in around six weeks.

Queens do not in general just die but they can be killed whenever we open a colony. They can drop off a comb and be lost on the ground. They can be crushed under the beekeepers foot without him/her knowing. They can be crushed between the frames or between a frame and a part of the hive. When you think of how often we open a colony and inspect the frames you realise how rarely a queen is lost in any of these ways.

The bees have a strange way of protecting their queen by "balling" her, a group of bees form a ball around the queen and suffocate her to death. Each of these is, in my view, a rare occurrence but it can happen and we should all be aware of this. Whenever the queen is lost the bees go into panic mode and they are seen running around the entrance looking for her. It is always worth checking around an apiary to see that all is well before leaving. If the queen is lost and there are young larvae in the colony then the bees will take action to rear a replacement but this takes valuable time.

Many researchers have estimated the number of eggs produced in 24 hours, these vary between 1000 and 2000 and it is very unlikely that the rate is constant over a period of hours or days. This gives the following results.

EGGS PER DAY	No. OF CELLS OCCUPIED BY BROOD	No. OF ADULT BEES ASSUMING SIX WEEK LIFE
1000	21000	42000
1500	31500	63000
2000	42000	84000

You could measure the total area of brood in one of your colonies and then calculate the number of cells occupied. It is possible to guess the number of bees in a hive. An estimate can be obtained by shaking ALL the bees into a container and weighing them. There are approximately 5000 bees per pound

The most accurate way is to kill ALL the bees and then count them!! Very counter productive.

No. OF CELLS IN COMMON BROOD FRAMES

WBC	10	45.000
National	11	50.000
Smith	11	50.000
British Commercial	11	70.000
Langstroth	10	61.400
Langstroth Jumbo	10	77.270
Dadant	11	85.000

These figures are taken from Thorne's catalogue.

(If you use the British Standard deep 14 x 12 multiply by 1.4)

God made the bees,
the bees make the honey.
We do the work,
the teachers get the money.

School child's lament

CHAPTER 3

Actually finding the queen

I can think of only three occasions when it is absolutely necessary to find the queen.

1. To mark her, this will make finding her easier next time but is no guarantee of being successful. When I was selling queens they were all marked in a three frame nucleus with a few thousand bees and I was not always successful in finding the queen.

2. To clip her wings, this is used to prevent the queen flying off with a swarm. The queen will then leave the hive and fall on the grass or in the undergrowth; hopefully the beekeeper finds her there and deals with the situation. If not then the swarm will return to the hive and not leave until a virgin queen emerges.

3. To destroy her. This is the ideal way to cull a queen. Below I will show you how these operations can be achieved without searching through the colony.

Actually finding queens in a colony. The odds are heavily stacked against you. Even small nuclei contain a few thousand workers; a full colony spring and autumn will contain 10,000 to 15,000 workers and, in the summer will contain 30,000 upwards.

A lot of bee books will tell you how to find the queen. Even with this information it is still like looking for the proverbial needle in the hay stack. Assume you have found the queen, what are you going to do next? If it is mark, clip or kill then the action is clear. Otherwise you will look at her but what can you tell from this viewing? Age, very doubtful unless she is marked with a colour that you have used and know. Her pedigree, very unlikely, her laying ability, the amount of brood and its layout will tell you a lot more. If we merely wish to know where she is then other methods are much quicker.

Finding queens is an acquired art, it can be learnt but as shown above is of little real beekeeping value. The best person I have found finding queens is a local commercial beekeeper, into dozens of colonies every day. He will regularly see the queen even when not looking for her.

If you must find the queen and do not wish to search for her then 'sieve' her out of the mass of worker bees. The combs having the bees on them are shaken into an empty box with a queen excluder fastened to the base. The sketch below shows a very good arrangement, it allows the combs to be slid under the excluder as they are shaken. The workers can then move back onto their combs so that the colony returns to normal as soon as possible. If the bees are reluctant to go down then a little smoke can be used to drive them down.

Once all the combs are shaken you can look for the queen on the surface of the excluder. This method does take a little time but you are almost certain to find the queen.

Queen Sieve

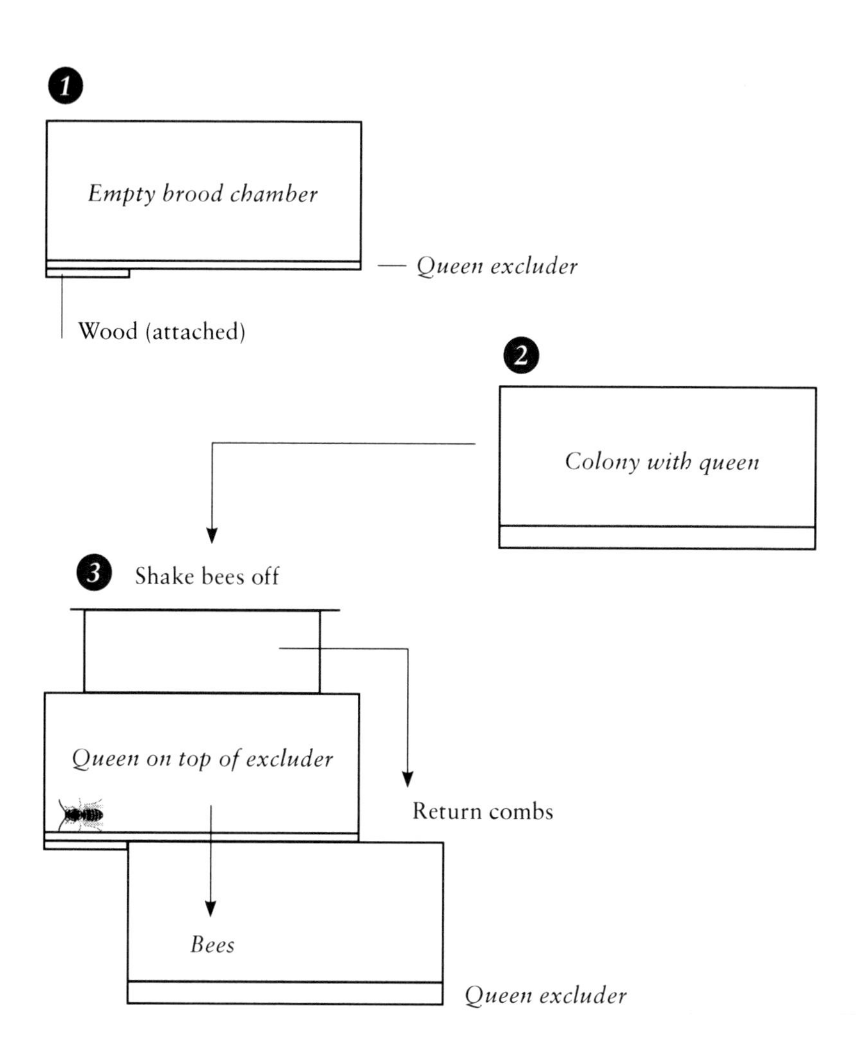
1
Empty brood chamber
Queen excluder
Wood (attached)
2
Colony with queen
3
Shake bees off
Queen on top of excluder
Return combs
Bees
Queen excluder

If you think you can you will
If you think you can't you won't
The man who wins is the
Man who thinks he can

Anonymous

CHAPTER 4

Queen excluders and includers

Queen excluders became more important when bar frame hives came into use during the 19th century. It was realised that the thorax of the queen is larger than that of the worker bees. An excluder could be made providing the gaps were large enough to allow a worker bee to pass but small enough to prevent the passage of the queen. The first excluders were made from wood, narrow strips were spaced correctly. Wood is not the most stable material so their efficiency would not be 100%. Next came narrow pieces of metal excluder between strips of wood.

Slotted sheet zinc then became common, these are good while they are flat but can distort while being removed. Zinc is soft and has a low melting point, steel and plastic have been available in more recent years, the trouble is that steel rusts unless protected and plastic has not been popular with the bees or the beekeepers.

In Britain wire excluders were first introduced by a firm called Waldron of Stratford upon Avon. They were efficient as an excluder but the wire was in the centre of the timber surround so the bee space could not be maintained in the correct position. I still come across examples of the Waldron excluder. More recently wire excluders made by Hoffman of Germany have become very popular; other manufacturers have now come to the market including one in Britain. Most of these have a bee space on one side only so that it is possible to have a correct space above and below the wires.

Wire excluders are more expensive but they do not easily distort and will last for 20, 30 or more years so are well worth the extra money. I recommend that you purchase the wire type.

Queen includers is a new term to me but is correct when the excluder is placed temporarily below the brood chamber to prevent the colony absconding. I now see that Mr L.E.Snelgrove used the word in his last edition of 'Swarming'. Absconding is a possibility when hiving a natural swarm or making a 'shook swarm', once there is brood in the colony the risk is negligible so the includer should be removed after a few days. Bear in mind that drones are also trapped in the hive while there is an includer under the colony.

Pieces of excluder are placed over the entrances of nuclei with virgin queens inside prior to artificial insemination. This was the situation in Brazil when a human worker removed the excluders and started off all the trouble with the 'killer bees'.

If you are ever short of queen excluders then a piece of plastic sheet can be placed over the brood nest. The colony and the queen will not split the brood nest into two parts. The plastic needs to cover two thirds of the top of the box, it is very successful.

CHAPTER 5

Swarming

Bees have been increasing the number of colonies by swarming for millions of years and we are not going to be able to breed this out no matter how we try. Some bees swarm more often than others and we are often urged not to breed from swarming colonies yet this is exactly the way most beekeepers increase the numbers of colonies that they keep. It requires considerable effort to do otherwise.

All the books on beekeeping give you a list of actions you can take to help avoid swarms, large brood box, early supers, ventilation etc, etc and still your colony swarms. I once had a three frame observation hive swarm and I have tried double brood boxes and lots of supers and they still swarm.

The age of the queen certainly has an effect, the older the queen the more likely the colony is to swarm. The logical conclusion is to only have queens which are one year old or less, this is very difficult to achieve.

There are lots of artificial methods of swarming control where the beekeepers makes the swarm on behalf of the colony , but they all start off 'Find the queen' and that is as far as many beekeepers get. Mr L.E. Snelgrove in his book 'Swarming' lists 18 different methods of dealing with a colony about to swarm, and there are many more.

Let us consider the probability of a colony swarming in an apiary of 10 colonies. In any year it is unlikely that all colonies will swarm or that none will swarm. It will depend on variables, some of which the beekeeper can influence.

1. The age of the queen. Colonies headed by young queens are less likely to swarm, as the queen gets older she produces less pheromone so the likelihood of the colony swarming increases.

2. The volume of the brood chamber. The larger the brood chamber the less likely the colony will swarm, within reason.

3. Storage space. Early addition of supers does have an influence.

4. The weather. Warm weather, cool weather, large amounts of nectar or poor nectar secretion all have an influence. During some seasons more colonies develop swarms than others and visa versa.

5. The input of the beekeeper. If they do nothing then this will have a consequence, some will swarm, others will not swarm. If the beekeeper takes steps to deal with any colony starting queen cells then the number of colonies which swarm can be reduced.

In a light swarming season may be only two or three colonies, out of the ten, will make preparations to swarm. In a heavy swarming season the maybe seven or eight colonies will colonies will make preparations. The beekeeper has options. The ideal is to check colonies regularly and deal with those colonies which produce queen cells and to leave those which do not; they are likely to produce the larger honey crops. When looking for queen cells it is not necessary to examine every frame in detail, if the first four or five frames have no cells then the rest are very unlikely to have cells.

Beginners find this period of the year very difficult. One has to decide which approach is best for them. You can do nothing and accept the consequences but this is not going to be very popular with your neighbours!!, you will also loose much of your honey crop. The other extreme is to be looking into the colony every day or so and try to make certain that the colony never swarms, this will be too much disturbance to the colony. To be successful the beekeeper must have a very clear knowledge of the swarming process and be clear in their mind of the action which they are going to take when queen cells are seen. This should be easier now that there is a method that does not require the beekeeper to find the queen.

Now that there are so few feral colonies swarms from this source will be much fewer in number than previously. It follows that most of the swarms which are now reported must come from kept colonies, i.e. mine and yours. If the 'shook swarm' method encourages more, even most, beekeepers to take charge of the reproduction in their own colonies then it must be very worthwhile. It should result in larger honey crops and less swarms to be collected from urban and rural areas. Castes or after swarms should become a thing of the past. Castes rarely make it through the first winter unless strengthened by the beekeeper, we would be better off without them.

In Chapters 10. and 11. I will outline methods whereby quality queens could be available. If this could be put into practice then it would improve all our beekeeping, how marvellous that would be.

We should all be aware of the recommendations of Mr J.W.Pagden. He put forward his views in a booklet in 1870 before bar frame hives were in general use. Many beekeepers hived a swarm on a new site as a matter of course; Mr Pagden said that moving the original hive aside and putting the swarm back on the original site would be an improvement. Over the next few days all of the flying bees would join the swarm increasing it's strength, at the same time the original colony was made smaller to help reduce the likelihood of castes.

This is good advice and should be put into practice as often as possible. Often a beekeeper is not aware which colony the swarm has come from. When we are making artificial swarms then the Pagden method can be put into practise.

The Pagden Method

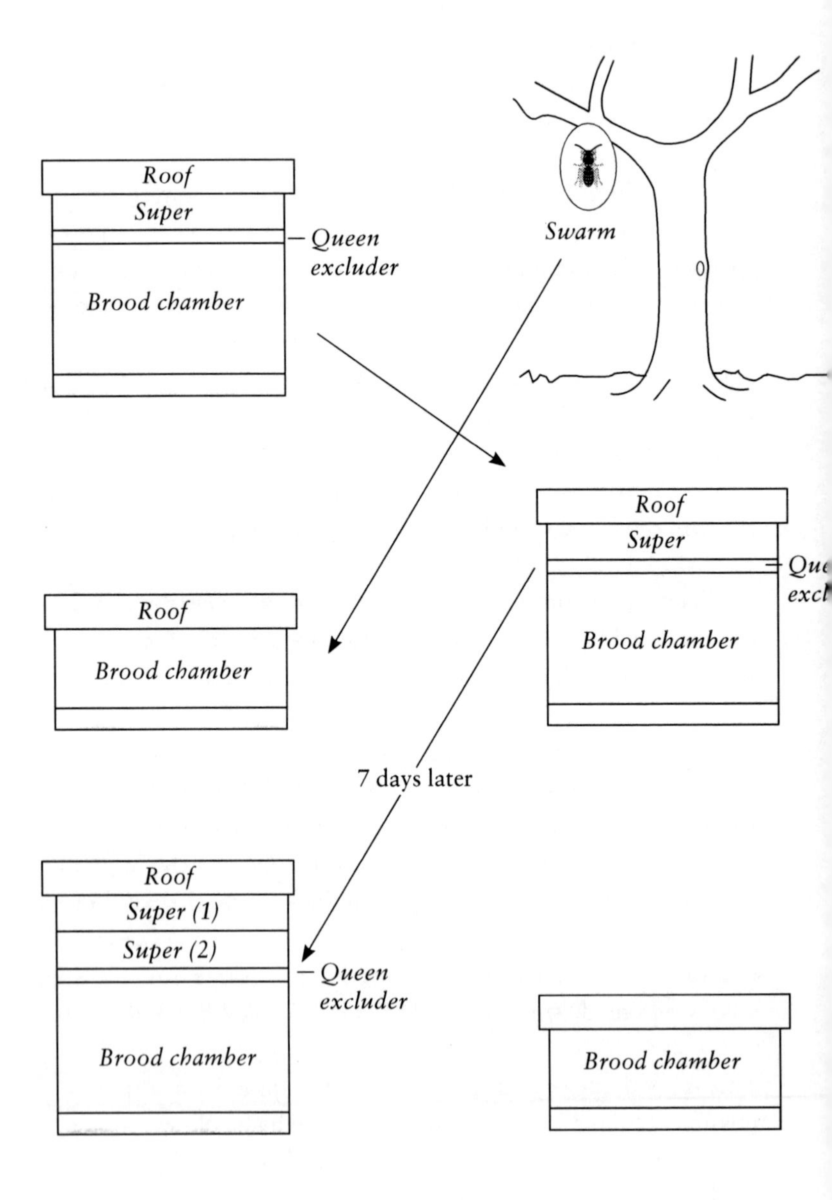

CHAPTER 6

Artificial swarming by the 'shook swarm' method

The biggest problem facing beekeepers new and old is that of swarming. There are several books written about the subject, lots of leaflets and articles without number in magazines. So what is the problem? To start with the beekeeper must fully understand the natural process. When ever you look into a colony and see queen cells then stop and ask your self "Exactly how far has the swarming process got?" "Is the queen still present?" "Have any virgin queens emerged yet?" If you are certain that the queen is still in the hive then you can proceed to make an artificial swarm. The main problem is that all the books say "Find the queen" or "Put the frame with the queen on into another brood chamber"

I recommend that you regularly read 'Controlling swarms and making increase' in Chapter 7 in Guide to Bees and Honey by Mr Ted Hooper. Study this chapter regularly until you fully understand the contents. The book in excellent and should be required reading for all beekeepers. I regularly dip into my copy bought in 1979.

When a person takes up beekeeping they are often shown a queen in a colony by an experienced demonstrator. They are tempted to think "If they can find the queen then I can find the queen" They try and are not successful, even after several attempts, so they give up. Beekeepers find this situation very frustrating. They know what they should do but do not have the knowledge or skills to carry it out.

The colony continues with its natural cycle and a swarm emerges from the hive. If the beekeeper sees this or is told where the swarm is clustered then he/she will be able to take action. If not then someone else will take the swarm or it will hive itself somewhere in time. The beekeeper has lost half of the colony and much of the possible honey crop. Is there a better way?

Over the past few years the National Bee Unit has been trying out the 'shook swarm' as a treatment for colonies with European Foul Brood. The bees are shaken off the combs and the latter are burnt.

In most cases the queen is found (by the inspector) and placed in a cage to be returned after the shaking has been completed. This is fair enough when the colony is diseased. This is regularly carried out with the assistance of the bee inspector

The 'shook swarm' method is mentioned in the book 'Swarming' by Mr L.E. Snelgrove. He does not think much of the method but it does lend itself to taking action without having to find the queen.

Where there is no disease the options are much better as the brood can be used to the benefit of the bees and the beekeeper. It is also the basis of several other possibilities. Some American beekeepers have been making 'shook swarm' into a shallow super [as a brood chamber] and then putting comb honey supers over this as a method of producing comb honey. On occasions I have made an artificial swarm by shaking all the bees off the combs in front of the hive and then letting the bees and the queen walk back into the hive. This has been on occasions when the queen could not be found. The result is a lot of bees out of the brood chamber, on the front of the hive and in the air. The shaken combs had to be put back on the top of the hive while the workers re- populated the brood area.

Prior to 2004 I had enjoyed 60 years of beekeeping without a serious disease problem. Then at the end of the summer in 2004 EFB was found in nine of my colonies. They were all treated with

Oxytetracyclin. A re check in 2005 found four colonies with EFB, three quite badly affected, all four were destroyed by burning. Two of these were at my request; I wanted to be as sure as possible that the problem was cleared up completely. I was told about the 'shook swarm' and this got me thinking. Would it be suitable as a method of making an artificial swarm to help so many beekeepers particularly those who have difficulty finding queens, definitely, "Yes"

A natural 'prime' swarm is composed of approximately half of the worker bees, the mature queen and some drones. If such a swarm is hived on foundation without supers then in a week or so most of the combs will be drawn. We should replicate this situation in the 'shook swarms'. If a prime swarm occurs early and given a good season some of these will produce a surplus of 30 to 60 lbs of honey and still survive the coming winter. An old saying:

A swarm in May is worth a load of hay
A swarm in June is worth a silver spoon
A swarm in July is only worth a fly
A swarm in August is worth a pint of sawdust
A swarm in September is something to remember
A swarm in October is rarely seen when sober
A swarm in November is as rare as one in December

This rhyme, from Skep days, is based on the prospect of surplus and the likelihood of the colony making it through the coming winter. Now a 'shook swarm' would consist of ALL the worker bees, the queen and all of the drones. A swarm of this size at the correct time should make a very good showing. The start of the natural swarming season depends on the spring weather but some swarms occur in April with the majority in May. By June and July it is mainly 'castes' and these are of little value on their own.

A prime or 'shook swarm' will be without brood in the combs so the older bees dying off will not be replaced for the next three weeks, the colony size will be shrinking. Against this a swarm has a lot of vigour, they are able to draw very good combs very quickly and the colony quickly regains its size once the new brood is emerging. Again a 'shook swarm' should be able to do even better because it contains more worker bees.

A natural swarm takes an amount of stores with it, this may be difficult to replicate in a 'shook swarm'. One possibility is to smoke the colony about 15 minutes before the work starts; this causes the workers to fill their honey stomachs in case they have to leave the hive, similar to a swarm. Feeding will be a must while the combs are drawn out.

A colony can start swarm preparations as soon as drones are seen on the combs. Ideally the beekeeper should see the start of queen cells, these are often play cells but they are the first signs of the preparation for swarming. This would be a good time to make the "shook swarm", it would be as near to the natural conditions as possible. Any earlier and the colony is still growing, much later and it may be too late. I am going to suggest that the period for shook swarms should be from the middle of April until the end of the first week in June, this must be tempered with due regard to the colony and the weather.

A queen includer under the brood box is to prevent the bees absconding. Sometimes a colony will just leave the hive for no apparent reason. The colony will not abscond if the queen is not able to accompany the rest of the bees. The queen includer should be removed after a few days, by this time there should be eggs and brood in the new combs.

IT MUST NOT BE LEFT IN POSITION FOR EXTENDED PERIODS.

Once the "shook swarm" is made we shall be left with a brood box of frames containing brood in various stages with the potential to produce approximately 30.000 new bees, but no covering bees. Place this over this colony if you only have one, for 24 hours. If you have more than one colony then the frames can be placed over one of your other colonies. Please see the following chapter for the reasons for this.

The advantages of this method are:

1. No need to find the queen.
2. The colony is placed on new combs.
3. The new frames need not be the same size as those from which the bees are shaken.
4. Good time to tackle European Foul Brood.
5. Good time to tackle Varroa.
6. Helps to reduce Nosema.
7. A good way to sell a colony. A 'shook swarm' is like a very big 'Package', these are very popular in America, Canada, Australia and New Zealand. Each 'Package' consists of two or three pounds of worker bees, a mated queen in a cage and a can of feed, all in a ventilated box. These are moved by road and air all over the world. They are used to start new colonies.

I hear and I forget
I see and I remember
I do and I understand

Anonymous

CHAPTER 7

Actually making a 'shook swarm'.

I anticipate that most beekeepers will read the whole of this book at some stage. I hope this will be the chapter that they turn to when they actually come to carrying out the process. If you are intending to make 'shook swarms' then I urge you to make preparations to have adequate equipment ready well in advance, say March time or before. The method does require extra equipment but no more than if you had caught a swarm and then hived it in your own apiary.

Have available:

1. A spare clean brood chamber, floor and queen excluder.
2. The required number of new or cleaned frames and new fresh foundation.
3. A spare or temporary floor, crown board and roof.
4. Some food, syrup, summer strength, or fondant.
5. Possibly an empty super box.

Before starting make sure you understand exactly what you are going to do. If it helps then make a dummy run away from the bees, affix a piece of paper on each box and write on the contents. If you make a mistake then little harm is done.

BEFORE YOU START MAKE ABSOLUTELY CERTAIN EVERYTHING IS READY.

FOR THE BEEKEEPER WITH ONLY ONE COLONY OF BEES

1. Remove the roof and crown board. Smoke the colony and replace the crown board. Leave for 15 to 30 minutes, during this time the bees will gorge themselves on food in the same way as a real swarm.

2. Remove the crown board; knock any bees on the board back into the brood chamber. Remove any supers and place to one side. Remove the queen excluder and knock the bees back into the brood chamber, the queen may be there. Place to one side.

3. Move the brood chamber and floor to one side or onto an upturned roof. Place a clean floor, a queen excluder and a clean brood chamber on the floor. Fill with new or clean frames fitted with new fresh foundation. If you prefer put an empty super over the brood box, I find it makes it easier to drive the bees down into the brood box. Lift the original brood chamber onto the top. Brush or knock the bees off the old floor onto the top of the old brood chamber, the queen may be there. Put the floor to one side.

4. If you know that there are queen cells on any of the old frames mark the top bar and DO NOT shake these frames, the bees must be brushed off. Use a bee brush, a soft hand brush, a large feather or a handful of long grass. The marking of the frames] could have been done at an earlier inspection.

5. Lift each frame in turn and either 'shake' or brush the bees down onto the top of the new frames below, it is not essential to remove every bee as the queen normally comes off at the first shake. Place each frame, free of bees, into a brood box or suitable box. When all frames have been dealt with, all of the bees will be on the tops of the new frames. Drive them down gently, with a small amount of smoke. When they are all down among the new frames remove

the old brood chamber. Now place a queen excluder onto the top of the new brood chamber and place the frames of brood and honey in a brood box on top of this queen excluder. If there were supers place them on top. Close up the hive and leave for 24 hours.

6. Now remove the box of old combs and supers], if in use, and place them on a floor on a site near the original site. Reduce the queen cells to one or two if you wish. If it is intended to go back to one colony then it should be only 4 to 5 feet away from the original hive with the entrance facing in the opposite direction. If it is intended to be for increase to two colonies then it can be further away 10 feet or more.

7. Once the old box of frames has been removed the 'shook swarm' should be fed heavily, even if there is a flow on. Once most of the new frames are drawn feeding can cease. Check the 'shook swarm' after 5 to 7 days to be certain that the queen is laying, if so this is a good time to remove the lower queen includer. When most of the new frames are drawn then the supers can be put back on the original colony.

8. Feed the box of old frames and brood. Leave for two weeks before checking to see if a laying queen is present. If not check again ten days later.

The 'shook swarm' should not require attention for the next three weeks while the queen refills the frames with brood. After that there is a remote possibility the colony will swarm again. Either do a seven to ten day inspection or accept that it might happen. Supers should be added as required.

Once the new colony has a laying queen it can be treated as a normal colony. If this colony is for increase then you are now looking after two colonies. If you wish to go back to one colony then you will need to unite them at the end of the season. If you are adventurous then consider a 'two queen' colony.

Making a shook swarm – for the beekeeper with one colony

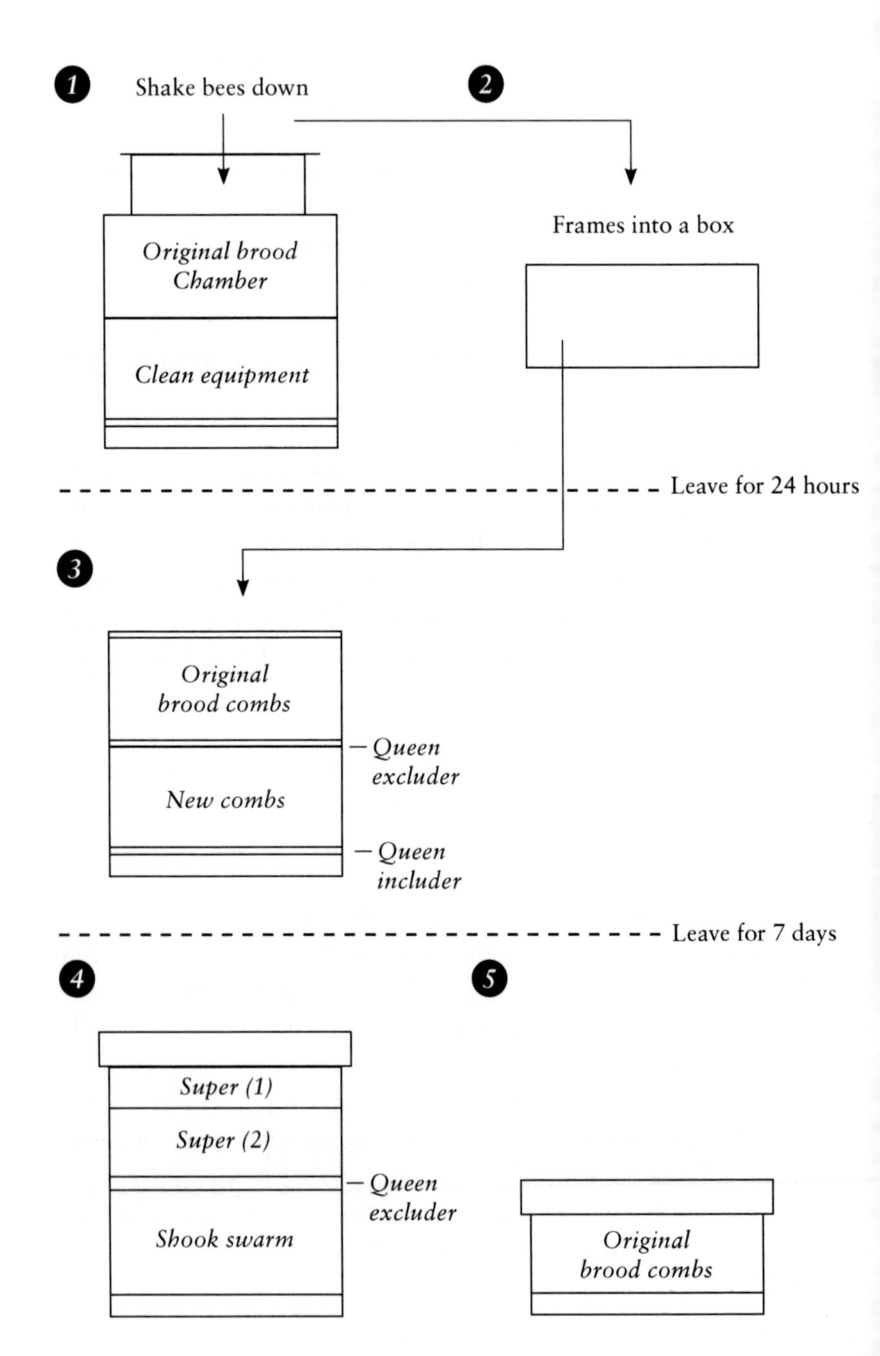

FOR THE BEEKEEPER WITH SEVERAL COLONIES

If you have more than one colony then the box of old frames and brood can be placed over any of your other colonies. Again put any supers on top of this hive. The 'shook' swarm should always be restricted to the frames of foundation only, so that they have no option but to draw out the new combs. This is the situation a natural swarm would be in once it has found a new home.

If you place a queen excluder between the colony and the box of brood without bees then all the brood will have emerged in 21 days. Without the queen excluder the queen will continue to lay over both boxes You will need to release any drones, emerging above the queen excluder, from time to time as they will be trapped.

Making a shook swarm – for the beekeeper with several colonies

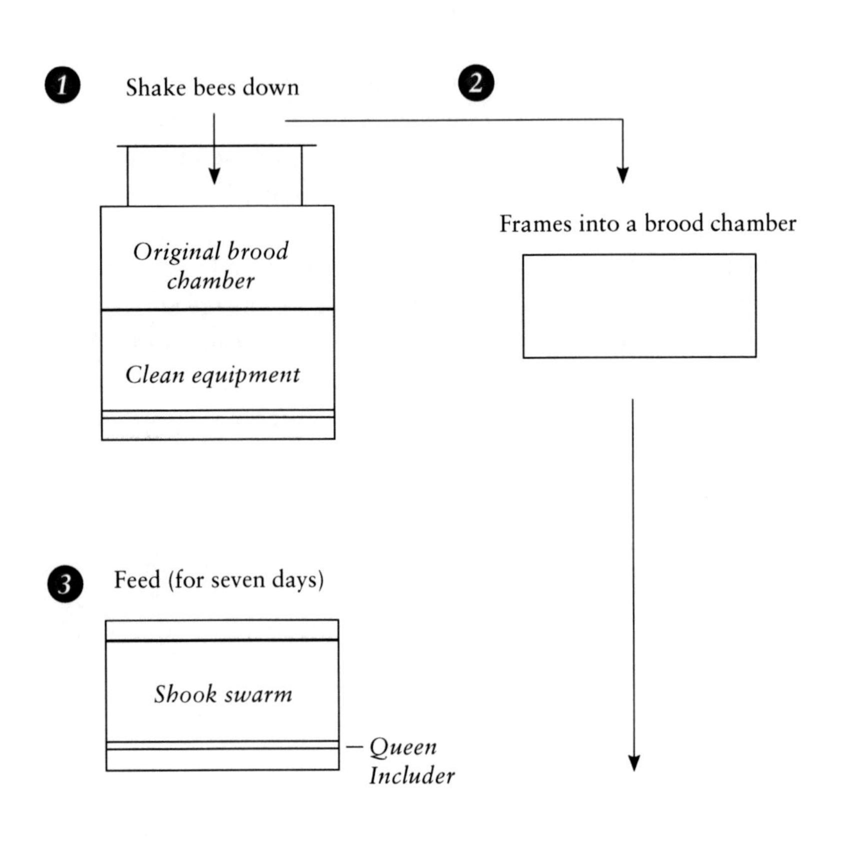

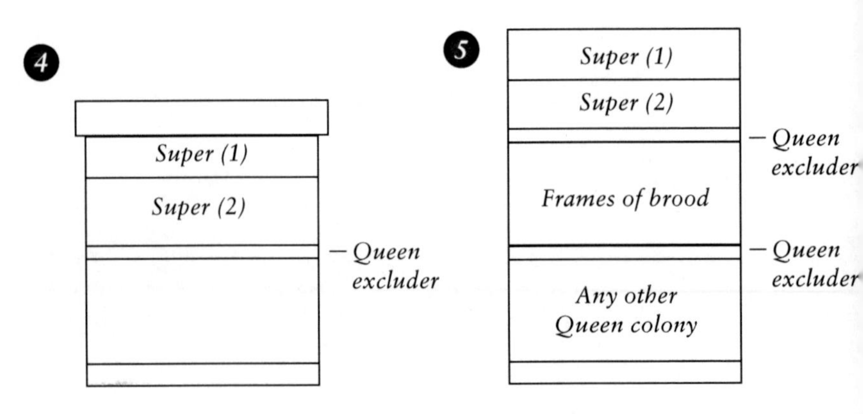

CHAPTER 8

The 'shook swarm' and disease

This is an excellent opportunity to deal with three of the most difficult bee disease problems which beekeepers have to face.

FOR COLONIES WITH EUROPEAN FOUL BROOD

As EFB is a notifiable disease your local Brood Disease Officer must be advised. He or she will assist with the 'shook swarm' and may well find the queen for you. Once the bees are removed from the frames the latter will be destroyed by fire. This method is considered to be 95% effective so your bees should be clear of EFB. If there is an amount of honey then this can be harvested with the approval of the Bee Disease Officer, and sold, it MUST NOT be fed back to any colony of honey bees.

If EFB is not suspected but your brood combs are very old then it may be appropriate to destroy them and the brood they contain as a precaution. The alternative is to place the combs over a queen excluder on another colony so that all the worker brood will emerge. After 21 days the combs may be burnt, rendered or used as seems appropriate. Old black brood combs are considered to be a potential source of EFB infection. We are being urged to change our brood combs more often and the "shook swarm" method is an excellent way of achieving this.

COLONIES AFFECTED BY NOSEMA

Changing bees onto a new set of combs will remove any Nosema spores from the brood rearing area, this should help the colony to be free of this disease in the near future. If the removed combs are to be used again then while they are empty they should be treated with acetic acid, to clear the spores.

FOR TREATMENT OF VARROA MITES

All colonies have Varroa mites in them; it is just a question of how many?

Once the adult bees have been separated from the brood combs then the Varroa mites will be very vulnerable. They can now only exist externally on the adult bees for the next nine days. This is an excellent time to treat with any appropriate medication, or as part of an Integrated Pest Management programme. Once larvae are at the point of being sealed the mites will enter the worker and drone cells and the opportunity will be lost.

If the brood combs, minus the bees, are placed over another colony then bear in mind that you will be adding all the mites within the sealed cells to those already in the colony. This may have a bearing on your Varroa treatment for this colony.

CHAPTER 9

Extended possibilities

Before using any of the methods below do be certain that all your colonies are free of any brood diseases. If you have more than one colony then any of the possibilities set out below are available to you.

Instead of putting the box of worker free brood combs over the colony from which they were taken they can be placed over another colony, with or without a queen excluder between. The bees from below will move up to look after the brood; they will be joined by approximately 1500 emerging workers each day. If there is a queen excluder between then all the worker brood will have emerged in 21 days time. If a queen excluder is not in place then the queen from below will lay in both boxes and it will become one larger colony.

With an excluder in position all the brood above will be sealed after nine days, it could then be moved to a new site and given a new queen, if available, or a 'ripe' queen cell, see Chapter 11. If neither of these options is available then a comb with eggs and young larvae should be provided for the bees to rear their own queen, this is the least desirable option. Feed.

In the same way this box could be split into two or three nuclei. Again a queen, cell, or frame of young brood must be provided. Feed.

If you really want to go to town then the frames from the two boxes can be made into four or five nuclei, one will contain the original queen and the rest will need a queen, cell, or frame of young brood. Feed.

Another possibility is to make a two queen colony. The book "A SIMPLE TWO-QUEEN SYSTEM" by Mr Ron Brown is excellent on this subject. Available from Northern Bee Books.

Are your larvae healthy

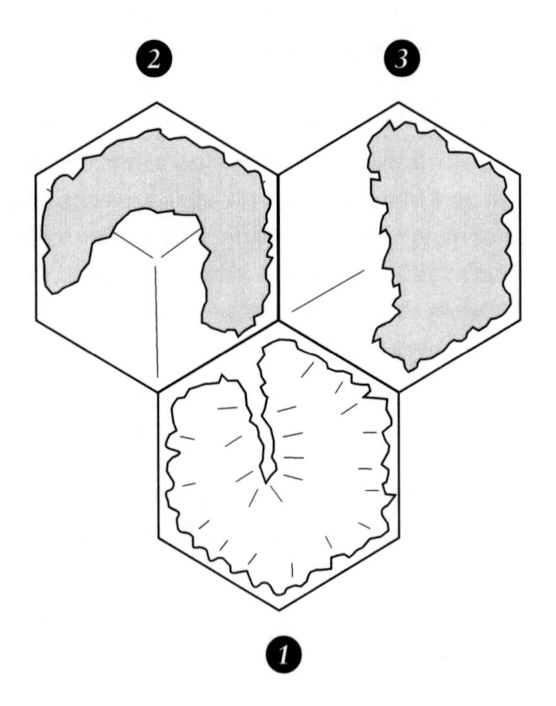

1. Healthy larvae, creamy white.

2&3. Larvae with EFB, yellow in colour and out of normal position.

MAKING NUCLEI

For many years all my nuclei boxes had fixed floors. Then I realised how simple it would be to make nucs if the floors were separate. So I recommend that you have this type. Mine are all half a brood box and take five frames.

Go to the colony from which you wish to make a nucleus, select the required frames and shake the bees from these back into the brood chamber. Place the frames into the nuc box(es) or brood chamber. Place a queen excluder over the brood box, with the queen in, and the boxes containing the selected frames over the excluder. Close up the hive, then 24 or 48 hours later lift the boxes from above the queen excluder and you have queen less nuclei ready to use as you see fit. Because of the queen excluder the colony queen must stay below in her own brood nest.

NOTE. If your nucleus boxes do have floors then either remove them or use a brood box to form the nucs and then transfer them to the nuc boxes.

Each nuc will require a queen, or a cell or be left to rear a queen. The general consensus is that nuclei are too small to produce worthwhile queens. Having made the effort to produce nucs then arrange for a queen or a cell to provide a queen. It will be worth the time and trouble.

MINI - NUCS

The big advantage of Mini-nucs is that they only require 500 bees for each unit. This means that many more queens can be mated from a given number of bees. As frames are not required these can stay in the colony to produce more bees. At a later stage the mated queens can then be united to a nucleus with frames and there will be no gap in the laying of fresh brood.

Making nuclei

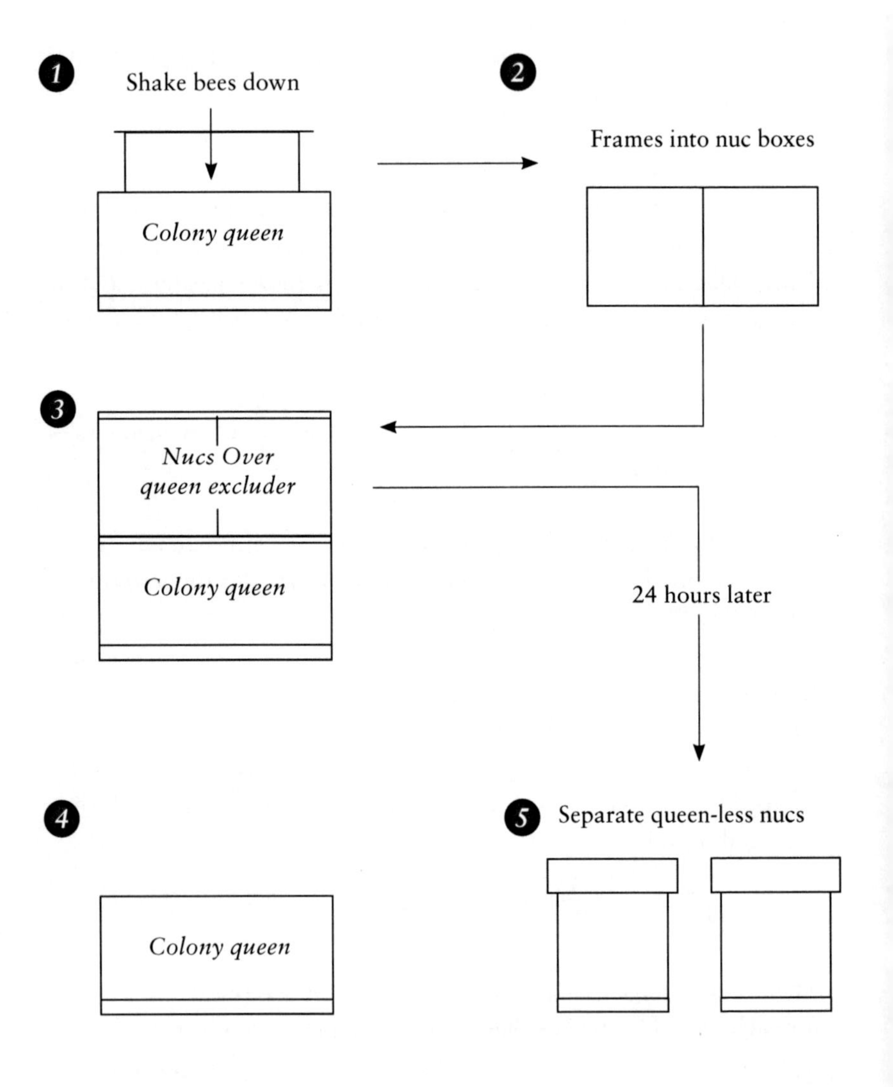

A while ago I made some Mini-nucs inside an empty four litre ice-cream carton. Pictures and details are below. In previous years I have tried these with bees from a honey super with variable success. This year I realised that I had a supply of young bees in the top brood chambers of brood from shook swarms. I was able to get some virgin queens from a colleague so I made up 8 mini-nucs from the bees and then added the queens, 4 of these mated and I was able to unite these to nucs made from the combs above a queen excluder. A 50% success rate may not sound very good but is comparable with normal nuclei on frames. One big advantage is that a mini-nuc contains only a few hundred bees whereas a nucleus on frames needs several thousand. Getting the queen mated from a mini-nuc and then uniting her to a larger nucleus is much more efficient.

In case you wish to 'have a go' I will describe the method I used in more detail. Have ready the mini-nucs with entrances closed and feeders full of fondant, the 'ripe' queen cells or the virgin queens. You will also require a honey bucket and lid or similar, a mist water spray and a scoop. I made my scoop from approximately half of a two pint milk carton, it worked very well.

USING QUEEN CELLS

Go to the colony [with the queen below a queen excluder] and smoke the top, remove the crown board and remove a frame, shake most of the bees into the bucket and spray them with water mist, place the top on loosely. Replace the frame and repeat until you have enough bees, it may have to be a guess the first time. You may have to spray the bees occasionally, this prevents them from flying but do not drown them. Close the colony up and move to the mini-nucs, this can be done under cover if desired. Open the top of a mini-nuc and take one frame out. Open the bucket and scoop up some bees, half fill of a one pound honey jar, this is about 500 bees. Pour the bees into the mini-nuc, add the 'ripe' cell, replace the frame and put the feeder on to keep the bees in. Close up and put in a cool dark place for three days. Release at dusk.

USING VIRGIN QUEENS

Now to introduce the virgin queens. Do be aware that virgin queens can fly!! If you wish to mark them this is a good time but do it inside! Have some one pound honey jars with the lids pierced for ventilation. Half fill each jar and put the lid on, leave for about 20 minutes while the bees realise they are brood less and queen less. Now pop a virgin queen into some just warm water, this will stop her flying and help the introduction. Open the Mini-nuc as above. Bump the jar to put the bees on the bottom, drop the queen into the Mini-nuc and immediately cover her with the bees from the jar. Replace the frame and feeder to close the nuc. Place in a quiet, dark place for three days and then release in the evening of the third day. Cross your fingers and/or any other token of hope you may have and leave for about 15 days, then check for eggs or brood.

You will find Ron Brown's book 'Managing Mini-nucs' of interest, it is available from Northern Bee Books.

UNITING TO A NUCLEUS WITH FRAMES

Make up the nucleus as described above. Close up the Mini-nuc and remove the lid. Remove the feeder and place a piece of news paper over the top of the frames, put in place the support for the frames. This prevents the frames dropping down. Turn upside down and place over the frames or the hole in the crownboard.. Place an empty box around the Mini-nuc and close up the hive. Allow two to three weeks before going into the bees. You will loose less queens this way.

INCUBATED BROOD

In the 1970's I was producing queens and nucs for sale. This required lots of mating nucs so a steady supply of bees is required. Once a worker cell is sealed it only requires keeping warm to come to maturity so sealed brood can be placed in an incubator. As I had never seen anything about this I made a temporary incubator with

Making a Mini-nuc, alternative method

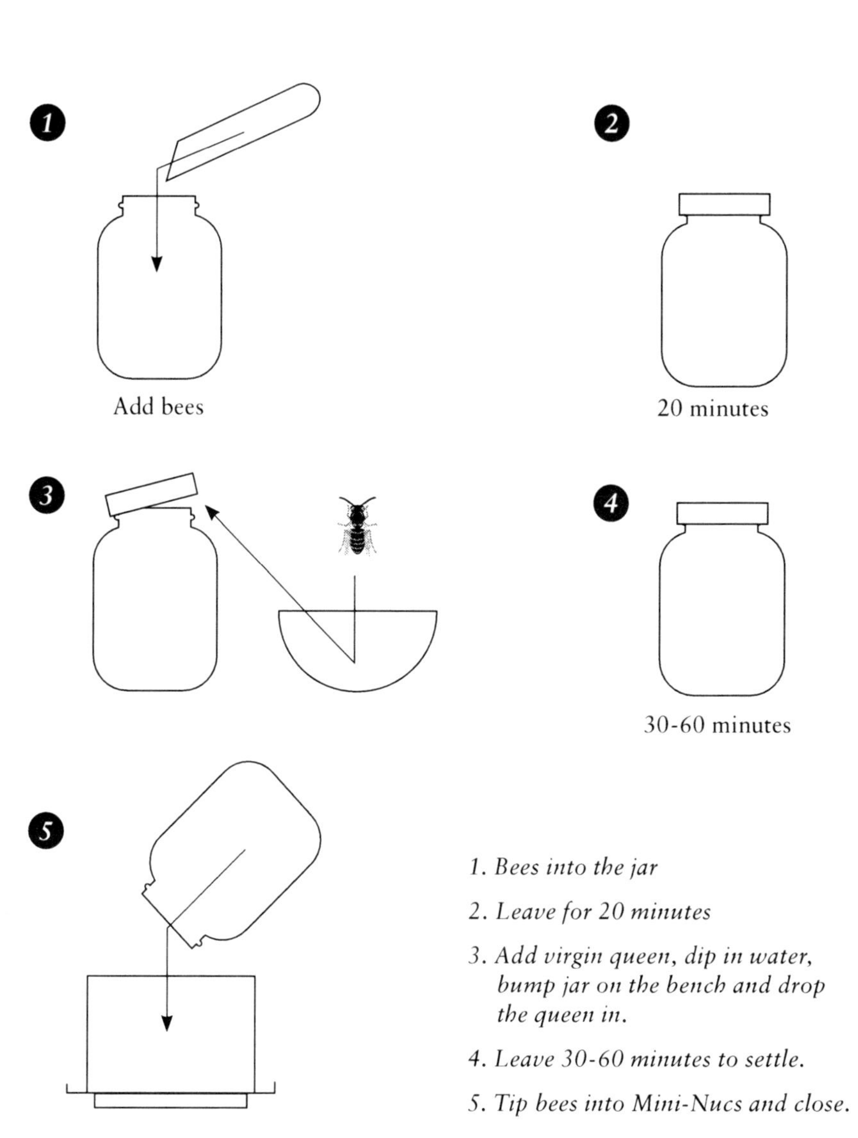

1. *Bees into the jar*
2. *Leave for 20 minutes*
3. *Add virgin queen, dip in water, bump jar on the bench and drop the queen in.*
4. *Leave 30-60 minutes to settle.*
5. *Tip bees into Mini-Nucs and close.*

four brood chambers, a fan heater and some blankets. It worked so I made a four foot cube with two inch blocks of insulation sandwiched between sheets of hardboard, a greenhouse fan heater with a thermostat to provide the heat and it all worked very well. A pan of water for humidity, a thermometer for temperature and a hygrometer for relative humidity completed the setup.

Brood frames of eggs and larvae were lifted above a queen excluder until all the cells were sealed, then into the incubator. Young bees were emerging daily and harvested every three days by shaking them off the frames into a plastic box; a light spray of water stopped most of them flying. As the young bees had never marked a site the nucs could be placed anywhere without loss of bees. The bees were dipped into one pound honey jars with ventilated lids and a marked virgin queen was added, a small "caste" was produced. This was left for a few hours and then transferred to a three frame nuc, placed in a dark quiet place for three days and then released at dusk. All my queen production was under my control until this time. The mating is now left to nature, the weather, and luck.

If you are an enterprising beekeeper and wish to try this on a small scale then you can set up an incubator as shown in the sketch. You will need ventilated covers on the top and bottom of the boxes containing the combs of brood so that the bees will not all fly out when you open the incubator. Blankets, Duvets or towels can be used as the outer insulation. A maximum minimum thermometer will enable you to monitor the temperature. It should be 93 degrees F (34 degrees C).

Simple brood incubator

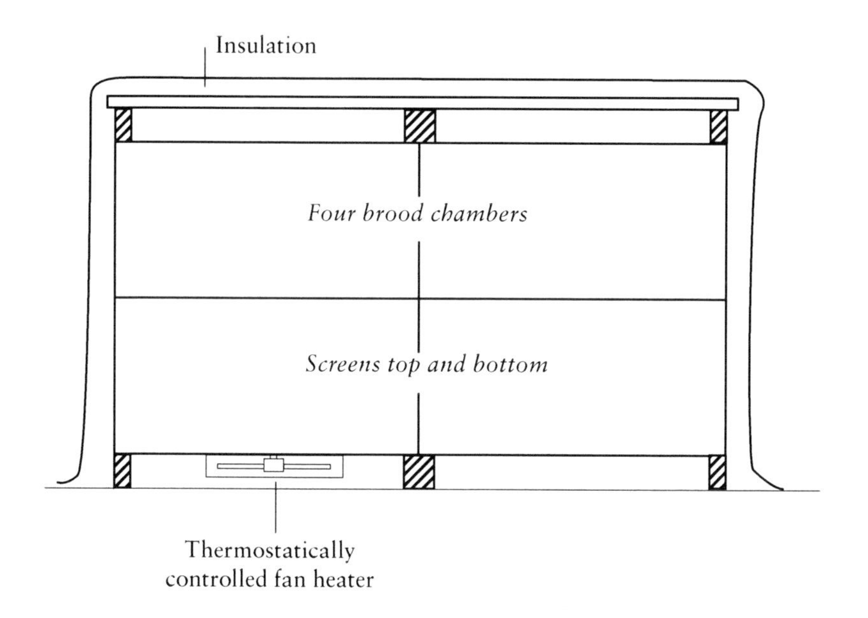

IF YOU ARE GOING TO SET UP YOUR OWN INCUBATOR DO GET A QUALIFIED ELECTRICIAN TO CHECK THAT ALL IS SAFE. YOU ARE GOING TO HAVE TO LEAVE THE HEATER RUNNING UNTIL YOU CLOSE THE SYSTEM DOWN.

By learning you will teach
By teaching you will learn

Anonymous

CHAPTER 10

Colony production and queen replacement

Both of these are areas which are neglected by many beekeepers. Establishing new colonies is generally left to collecting swarms. In some cases the beekeeper will be aware that the swarm is from one of their own colonies, otherwise the swarm will be of unknown origin. A few beekeepers make a conscious effort to produce nucs and then develop these into colonies. Very few of these make an effort to produce queens and then cull the poorest of the queens.

I hope that the ease of making artificial swarms by "shook swarming" will encourage more beekeepers at least to take on the production of their own replacement colonies. Yes, it requires some effort but the result must be worthwhile. The arrival of Varroa has meant the more frequent loss of colonies, sometimes a few at a time and on occasions in larger numbers. It is this which made a good number of beekeepers "give-up" their beekeeping in the 1990's. Once you lose all your colonies it requires real determination to start again.

If every beekeeper started just one more colony than they really required each year and then culled the poorest just think how much improvement this would produce.

With queen replacement the position is more complicated. At the moment most beekeepers rely on swarming or supersedure in established colonies. Where a colony has swarmed then a replacement queen will be reared by the bees remaining. Supersedure queens are considered to be very good but most of us are unaware that the process has taken place. It happens at a time of the year when we do not look into our colonies so often. Unless the previous queen was marked or clipped then it will be impossible to know that a queen has been superseded.

Another method is to purchase a new queen and introduce her to an established colony or a nucleus. The prospect of a new queen and a new strain is attractive. Many of the queens available are imported. queen production in Britain is very difficult, our weather is not very dependable and the season is short. Some years it is possible to start in April but numbers will be small, later in the season larger numbers are possible so some queens are available which have been produced in Britain

Many beekeepers are of the opinion that well bred queens from your own colonies are often as good as or better than any that you can purchase. Yes, it does take an effort but the results can be very satisfying.

CHAPTER 11

Queen rearing

On a small scale, say up to 20 colonies this is quite difficult and very time consuming. Most of the methods recommended rely on the bees producing cells along the edge of a piece of natural comb, the problem then is to divide the cells into singles without damaging the wax body of the cell.

In the 1970's I taught myself to graft and produce queen cells. After many setbacks I succeeded. Grafting needs a steady hand and reasonable eyesight, with spectacles if necessary. I started off using a Morris Board, later I used the swarm box as a starter box. This is a ventilated nucleus box with access for frames at the top but no entrance for the bees. My method was to develop a double brood box colony as early as possible. A few days before the first graft shake the bees down into the lower box and place a queen excluder between the two, the queen is now below the excluder. On graft day take the swarm box and insert two frames of honey and pollen [no brood] and a frame feeder of weak syrup. Now shake the bees from 3 to 6 frames from the top box into the swarm box. A funnel helps but is not essential. The swarm box now contains several thousands of brood-less and queen-less bees. Leave for 2 to 6 hours, by this time the bees will have realised their hopeless plight and be roaring.

Make the graft [or similar, see below] and place the frame of cells into the swarm box, place it in a cool quiet position for 24 hours.

Much is made of the risk of chilling the larva in books on queen rearing. I hope I have always been reasonably careful and I have never had a problem. In a book I read a while ago the author spoke of a frame of grafted cells which was left out all night be mistake. This frame was put into a swarm box the following morning and there was a good take of cells. The frame now needs to go into a rearing colony and the top of the double brood colony is ideal. Lift the frame out of the swarm box, take a few minutes to see how your graft has gone, turn it over, all the accepted cells will have a larva in a pool of Royal Jelly and new wax around the cell edge. Now place the frame into the centre of the top box of the rearing colony, close up the frames and feed. In five days the cells will be sealed and by day 10 the cells will be 48 hours from emergence, they are said to be "ripe" and should be distributed to nuclei. A strip of aluminium foil, 1/2inch by 3 inches wrapped around the body of the cell will act as a protector until the virgin queen emerges.

If you wish to try queen rearing without grafting then there are many more methods of providing larva of a suitable age for the bees to rear as queens. Try one or more. If you have an incubator then the cells can be placed in there when sealed, each cell needs to be in a separate container to keep emerging queens apart, otherwise you will only have one queen!! These virgins can be introduced to small groups of queen-less and brood less bees as described earlier..

I used one of my bee houses [see Beecraft May 2003 and Chapter 12] and an incubator so that I could work inside until the queens were all emerged. It was not until the nuclei were ready to be put outside that the weather became of any consequence. I found this very satisfactory.

Ripe queen cells are very easy to move about. queen cell carriers operating at 12 volts are available for use in a car using the cigar lighter socket. I have a queen cell carrier, the case is a domestic cool box and heat is from car bulbs.

Ripe queen cells could be available on a weekly basis from mid April until the end of June, this would be an easy way for any beekeeper to access better quality queens, they can be introduced into nuclei or allowed to emerge and then added to queen-less and brood-less bees. Associations could provide guidance and demonstrations. In the first year the virgin queens will mate to local drones, the following year the drones from the new queens will be of the same type, from then on the drone pool in the area will all be similar. This would auger well for the progeny to follow.

Mated queens are too cheap considering the trouble and effort to produce them. I suggest a price of £20.00 for mated queens and £5.00 for queen cells. 2007 values.

Quiet calm deliberation
Disentangles every knot.

Harold Macmillan

CHAPTER 12

Keeping bees inside

Like many other beekeepers I had often thought that bees could be kept inside to the benefit of both the beekeeper and the bees. Attempts between the 1940's and the 1970's showed that the main problem is getting the bees to find their way outside again, also the amount of light available, this is not sufficient to see the contents of the frames. As you will see below eventually I found a way which overcame both of these problems.

In 1944 my father had an observation hive made, six British standard brood frames and two shallows above as shown in 'Beekeeping New and Old', by Herrod Hempsall, it was very large and heavy, but that is another story. We lived near the centre of Birmingham and the only way we could have bees at home was for them to be upstairs so that they flew out over the small back garden. It was decided that the observation hive should be on a table with the bees going under a sash window, this was in my bedroom! The main problem occurred when the hive was opened; a few bees would end up on the floor. Later I had bees in a shed, to try my hand at queen rearing, with the usual problems, firstly it is quite dark and one cannot see down into the cells, the other major problem is that the bees that fly off the combs fly to the windows and cannot find a way outside. Later I felt there had to be a better way to get enough light onto a bee house. I had seen the inside of a number of touring caravans with lantern roofs; these seemed to be the way to go. I had also seen poultry houses which could be pulled around a field by a tractor. These gave me an idea for a mobile bee house. It would be built on two skids so it could be moved and loaded onto a trailer, as far as I know no-one ever used this part of the idea. The design had entrances through the solid plywood sides and a lantern roof to provide an escape for the bees, ventilation and light. I was living in Lancashire at the time and selling equipment for Thorne's so I built the first one and put it on display. Over the next 10 years I sold about 12 of these bee-houses and the customers seemed very pleased.

The most popular was the 8' by 6'; the 8 feet length would accommodate four colonies on two levels on each side. 16 colonies in 48 square feet is very economical of floor area. The frames were the warm way to make removal easier. Each group of four colonies were housed in a single unit i.e. four brood chambers between two side members, again of plywood. Supers of light weight construction were used with a crown board, no roof was needed.

The light inside is excellent, like daylight even on a dull day. I even did my grafting inside the bee-house, quite warm and no wind. This enabled all the operations required in queen rearing from grafting up to the point where the nucs are placed outside to be carried out within the bee house and independent of the weather. This is a worthwhile point where operations must be carried out to a set time-table.

The main advantages are that the flying bees are not aware that the beekeeper is there. You can open the colony without bothering about the flying bees, returning foragers are unaware of the beekeeper and bees that leave the combs fly quickly to the light above and then escape. You can work in the rain and wind and the bees do not seem to be upset. In a built up area the neighbours are not aware that there are bees in the bee-house. The late Mr Ted Crimmins of Southport wrote an article in Beekeeping Quarterly some years ago, he was very close to his neighbours and put a nylon mesh screen around the front about four feet away so that the bees had to fly upwards and so over the surrounding gardens.

If a colony became queen-less the workers could be seen walking across to the next queen-right colony and joining them. I have seen dividers on the front of some continental bee-houses which presumably prevent this happening. The bees seemed to winter inside as well as outside but of course the individual colonies could not be 'hefted' so food reserves had to be judged by eye. Honey crops were no larger as this depends on forage. Theft of individual colonies would be prevented and vandalism less likely.

I never found it too hot inside but if this is found to be a problem then a ventilation panel at low level would provide a through passage of air.

I have plans for a 4' and 6' to take eight colonies, a 6' by 6' to take 12 colonies and the 8' by 6' for 16 colonies. The construction was ply on an external framework for the walls and board and felt for the roof. The floor was ply on a framework of beams. The door should be wide enough to carry a brood box through with space for your hands as well!

If any reader should like a set of the plans then I will provide these at a cost of £5.00 per set.

Where ever you keep your bees do enjoy your hobby.

All photography by Lewis Mann

Under construction - floor and blank end

Under construction - floor, end and sides

A completed 8' x 6' beehouse

Four brood chambers under construction

Four brood chambers (showing two layers)

Beehouse ready for bees

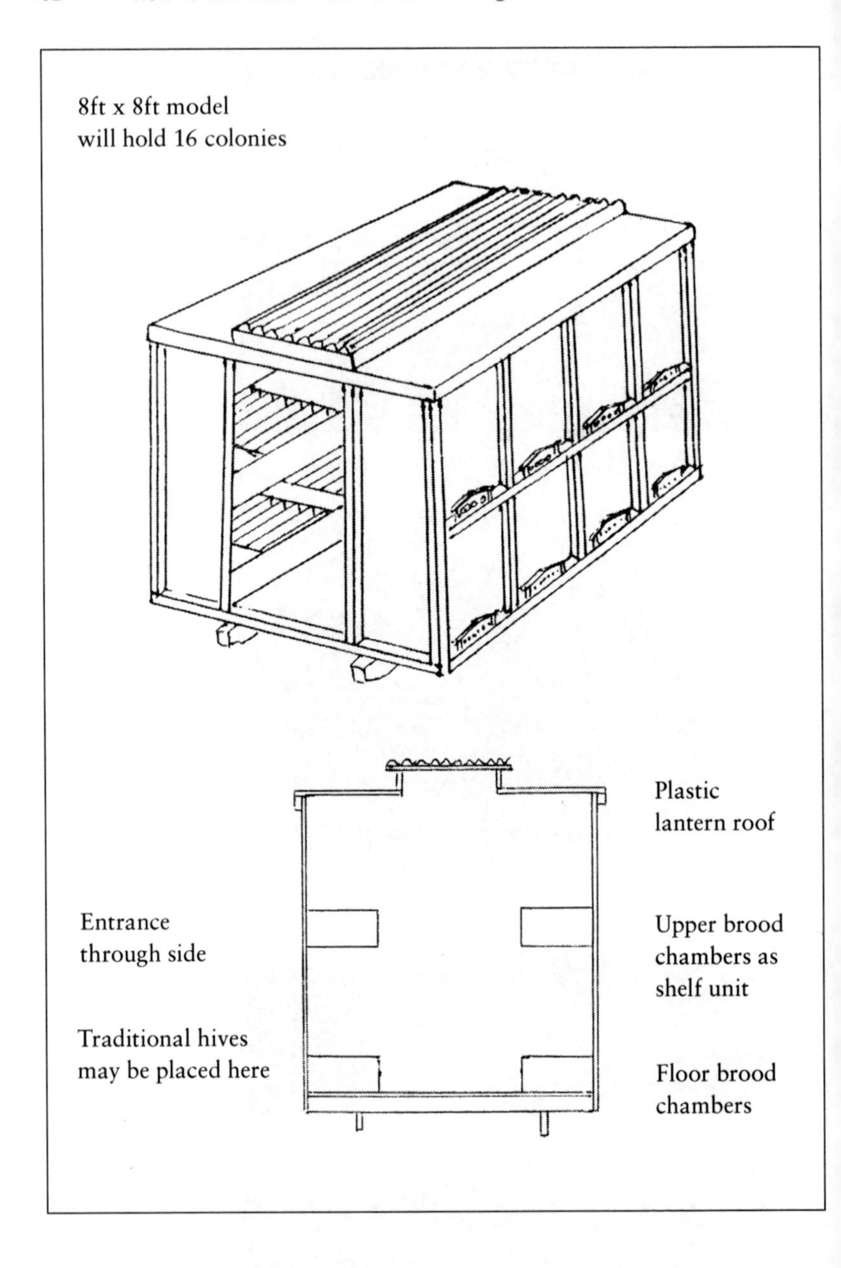
8ft x 8ft model
will hold 16 colonies
Plastic
lantern roof
Entrance
through side
Upper brood
chambers as
shelf unit
Traditional hives
may be placed here
Floor brood
chambers

CHAPTER 13

Mini-nucs to make

From what has gone before you will see that I am quite happy to make something myself if I think it may be better or different. Mini-nuc boxes are available from the manufacturers but they cost £10.00 to £20.00 each. They are only useful during the summer. Around the turn of the century I had an idea that it would be possible to make a Mini-nuc in a 4 litre ice cream container. These are used by ice cream outlets to serve into cones; most shops ask 10 pence for the empty ones. Eventually I set on the one you will see in the plan and pictures. These function quite well and the skill seems to be in preparing the bees and cell or virgin queen.

The very big advantage is that it only requires 500 bees [about half a one pound honey jar] to make a caste to which can be added a cell or virgin queen. If a unit fails then the bees seem to find their way back into another colony and you are left with an empty Mini-nuc box. With a nucleus on frames any that fail are likely to get laying workers which ruins the comb for further use. Mini-nucs are almost throw away.

Once a young queen is laying it is easy to unite it to a normal nuc on frames, this eliminates the introduction of the queen. The nucleus can than either be used to introduce the new queen into an existing colony or built up into a new colony. The cosy shown is a piece of old carpet cut to fit over the top of the box, it is held in place by a piece of wire to hold it to the box.

You are welcome to copy the plan (see pages 66 and 67). Photocopy from the book and then increase to double size to make it readable. Making these Mini-nuc boxes is an ideal task for winter days and evenings. A container of fondant will last two to three weeks and can easily be changed for a full box if necessary.

The only snag I have found is that it is difficult to open if the bees inside are queen less as they all come flying out. This can be overcome by putting the cell or virgin queen in with the bees when it is loaded.

Photo: Lewis Mann

Mini-nuc cosy

Photo: Lewis Mann

Mini-nuc assembled

Photo: Lewis Mann

Detail of entrance

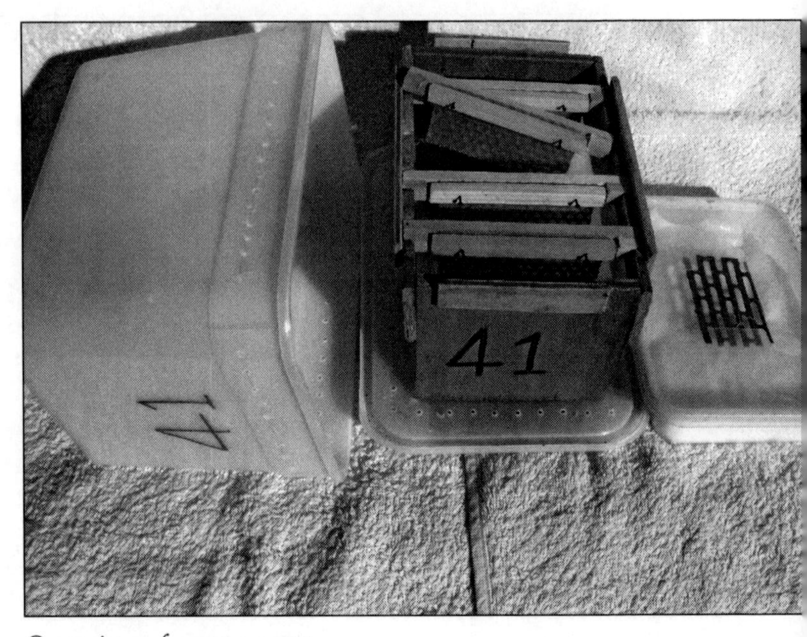

Overview of components

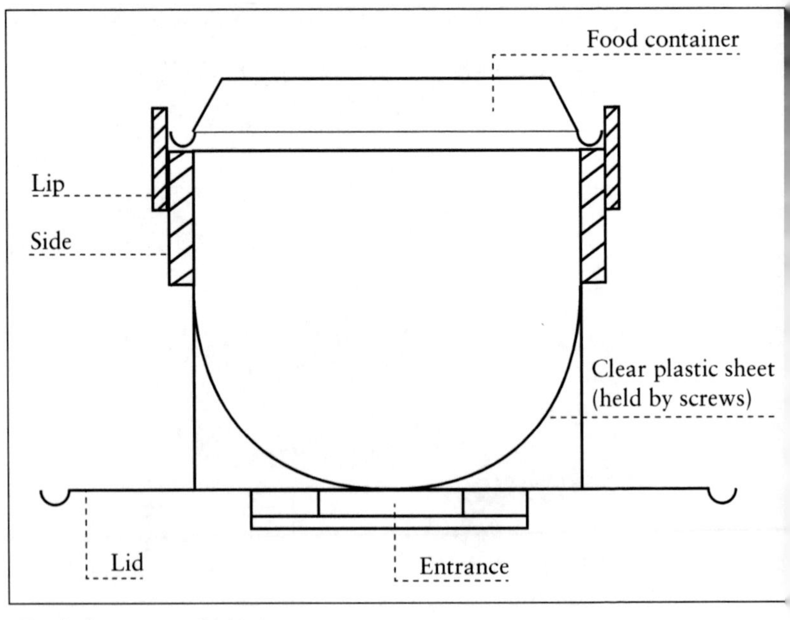

End elevation of Mini-nuc

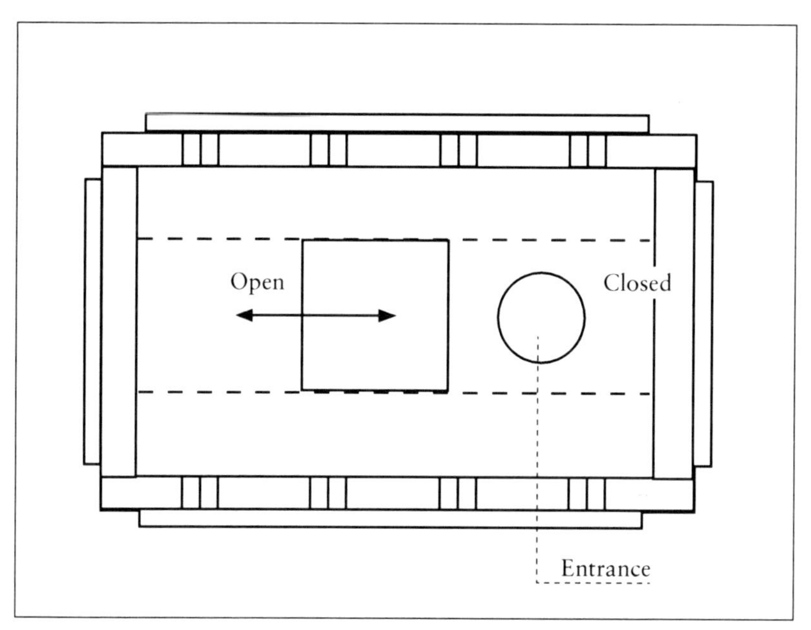

Plan view of Mini-nuc

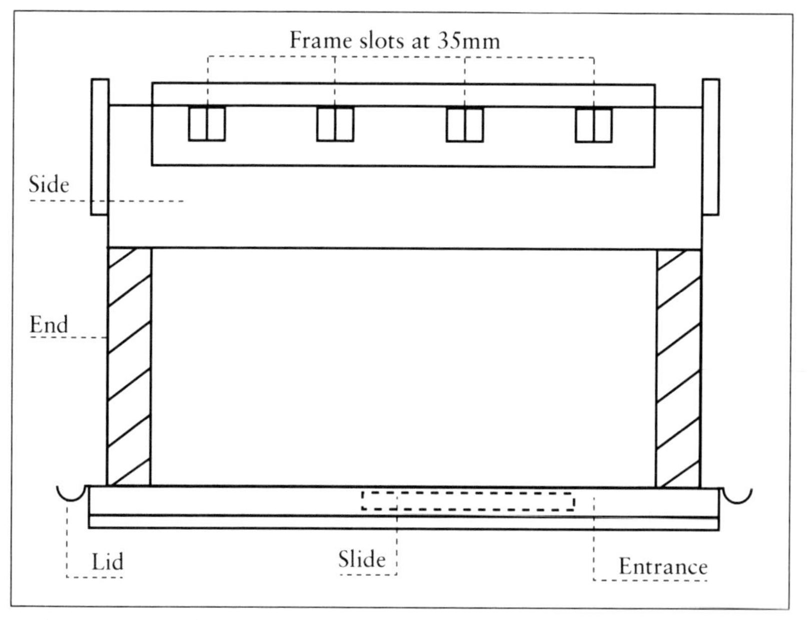

Side elevation of Mini-nuc

Mini-nuc construction notes

– The Mini-nuc is built inside a four litre plastic ice cream container.
– The feeder is an A500 take-away container.
– The frames are top bars only.

Cutting List

Ends: 110mm wide x 100mm high (9mm ply)

Sides: 175mm wide x 40mm high (6mm ply)

Plastic sheet: 210mm wide x 297mm high (A4)

Entrance base: 205mm x 90mm (6mm ply)

Entrance sides: 90mm x 25mm x 10mm

Slide: 60mm x 48mm (9mm ply)

Lips: Thin material to keep feed central, top bars made from frame, bottom bars are small pieces of foundation as starters.

CHAPTER 14

The future of beekeeping

When my beekeeping started it was possible to use the 'let alone method'. Place one or more beehives at the bottom of the garden and wait for a swarm to occupy the hive, place supers on and harvest the honey in August. These colonies could be left to winter and the process would be repeated the following year. If a colony died out then it was very likely to be replaced by another swarm later that year.

In 1992 Varroa arrived and 'let alone beekeeping' became a thing of the past. Feral colonies still exist and may live for a few years but in the end Varroa will get them, there are now far fewer feral colonies about.

During the past five years I have been involved in a beginner's day each April. The numbers coming forward have been surprising and females have been the greater proportion. These new beekeepers will take Varroa in their stride as they have not known a time without the mite. Without treatment a colony will succumb to Varroa or a virus associated with Varroa in four to five years.

I hope this book will help beekeepers new and old to cope more readily with swarming and as a result improve their bees and beekeeping. I am going to make three wishes for the future. If I can find a way I will call back in 100 years time to see how things have changed.

1. I would like to see a National Bee Breeding Programme; many other countries have such a scheme. At the moment large numbers of mated queens are imported from around the world, these are of assorted types and then join our national gene pool, this cannot be good for the future of our beekeeping.

Such a scheme should be organised jointly by the BBKA and the Bee Farmers Association, both would benefit. It is most likely that only a Bee Farmer would have a large enough group of colonies to make selection and testing possible. I do not think it would be viable to produce mated queens in sufficient numbers for sale. This requires a very large number of mating nuclei and equipment plus some very dedicated operatives. Our season is too short.

A more practical scheme would require a breeding establishment to produce a number of breeder queens probably on a National scale. These queens could then be used by a good and dedicated beekeeper to producing queen cells in bulk. These could then be purchased and used by beekeepers small and large; this would be big step forward. In the first year the virgin queens would mate with the drones of the area, for subsequent years there would be an increasing concentration of drone from the stock being propagated. I suggest a price of £5.00 per queen cell, [2007] this would give a return to the cell producer and some finance to the National body looking after the scheme.

2. I would like to see beekeepers have to register nationally; this would help with disease control. No one gives their bees disease deliberately, it always comes from another diseased colony or equipment and we have no control over these. It would enable the inspectors to cover an area more effectively. A register would probably increase association membership and as a result increase numbers for the British Beekeepers Association. The B.B.K.A. is our national voice for all things to do with beekeeping, the stronger the better.

3. We have far too many types of hive in Britain. Each type has a history and a following of beekeepers who feel it is ideal for them. In most cases they followed a helpful beekeeper or obtained their first bees on that type of frame and once started it is very difficult and expensive to change.

I wrote a lengthy article which appeared in Beecraft August 2004 where I set out my thoughts. The world is becoming a global village and the most common hive in the world is the Langstroth so I feel this type should become our normal and "National hive" within Britain.

One last comment, "Once you have the disease of beekeeping in your blood it is very difficult to remove so do enjoy your hobby. Although bees are very small we are in awe of them and they will provide you with challenges and interest for the rest of your life."

HAPPY BEEKEEPING.